W9-CQS-500

Tapping Play™
Creates Your Happy Rainbow Day

Listen to song clip at Tappingplay.com

Copyright © 2011 Text, Illustrations, Lyrics and Melodies by Debbie Teichmann

Published and printed in the United States

Annabelle   Billy   Franny

TAPPING PALS

What is Tapping Play™?
Tapping Play is the daily celebration of your beautiful and unique child through the act of singing and tapping!

Are the book and songs used each day?
Yes! The book and songs are set up with 7 sections (Monday through Sunday). It takes 3 minutes each day with your child to sing and tap your way to a fun and happy rainbow day.

What is the song teaching my children?
Tapping Play helps teach your children to love themselves and be able to verbalize it! The song's daily verses emphasize positive thoughts, affirmations, and happy hugs.

What age is appropriate for this book and song?
This upbeat song of love and celebration has no age limit. It brings happiness and joy to all age groups – young and old. We encourage you to join your children and sing and tap daily!

What is Tapping?
Meridian or Energy tapping is part of the Emotional Freedom Technique (EFT). Tapping on meridian points can help reinforce our daily positive messages. For more information on EFT, please refer to our website: **tappingplay.com**

How do my children and I learn the tapping points?

Please refer to our page named Tapping Points where Billy and Franny are demonstrating each of the individual tapping points. Your child should use their waving hand. For easy use, the words of the song are color coded to match the corresponding tapping heart points on Billy and Franny. An instructional video is also available on our website Tappingplay.com.

What if my child is tapping on the wrong point?

Relax! Tapping on any point can have benefits. Tapping Play is designed to be fun and carefree. Your children will develop the skills and timing through daily repetitive use. There is no right or wrong way!

Can very young children benefit from Tapping Play?

YES, YES, YES!!!! Singing, dancing, hugging and/or tapping on any point is perfect. Young children learn from watching and repetition. There is no right or wrong technique. Your beautiful little free spirits know what feels good and happy and will create their own technique.

Is a video available?

On our website you will find the main sign-in page; FREE daily song download information (use coupon code "HAPPINESS"); an instructional Tapping Play™ video, free coloring sheets along with other resources. Tappingplay.com

P
A
R
E
N
T
S

Use Your Waving Hand

Point 1

EYEBROW

Point 2

SIDE OF EYE

Point 3

UNDER EYE

Point 4

UNDER NOSE

Point 5

CHIN

Point 6

COLLARBONE

Point 7

UNDER ARM

Point 8

TOP OF HEAD

(HUG)

TAPPING POINTS

(We will use Monday 1 and Monday 2 as our example)
Open the book to Rainbow Monday 1 and Mp3 track 1.

Verses 1 & 2

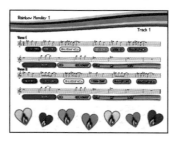 

The words are color coded and correspond with the tapping point heart colors.
Annabelle expertly creates our Word of the Day in beautiful rainbow colors.
Billy and Franny playfully demonstrate the colored tapping points.

Turn to Rainbow Monday 2.

Verses 3, 4 & 1

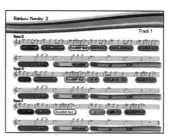 

Annabelle, our free spirited tapping guide.
Lovingly guides Franny who is tapping on her eyebrow point.

Join Billy on the right as he demonstrates Verse 1 words and tapping points

Use Your Waving Hand

Point 8 AND COMPLETELY

I AM FREE Point 1
BEING ME Point 2
I'M A HAPPY CHILD Point 3
I AM FREE Point 4
BEING ME Point 5

I'M A HAPPY CHILD Point 6

I DEEPLY Point 7

LOVE MYSELF
(HUG)
Point 9

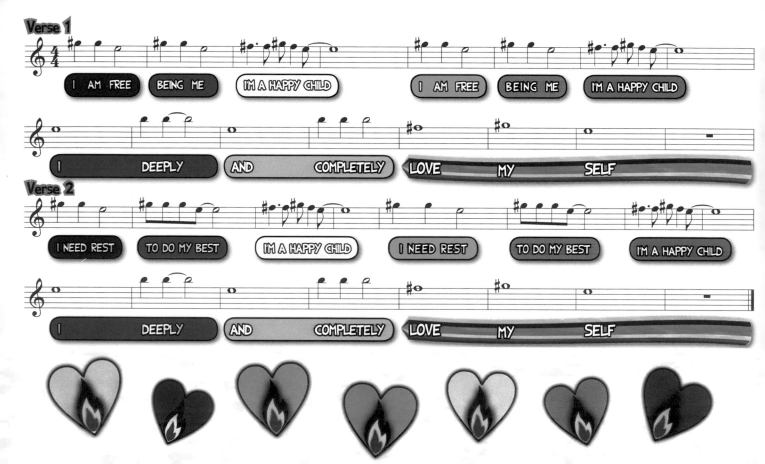

HAPPY

MONDAY 1

Rainbow Monday 2

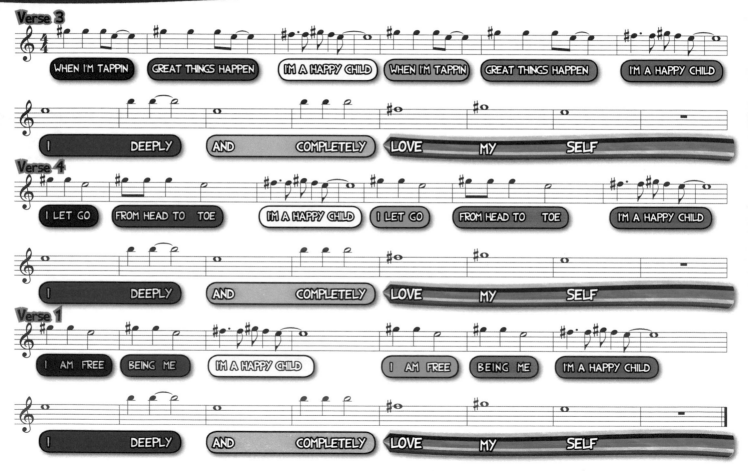

HAPPY

EYEBROW
Point 1

MONDAY 2

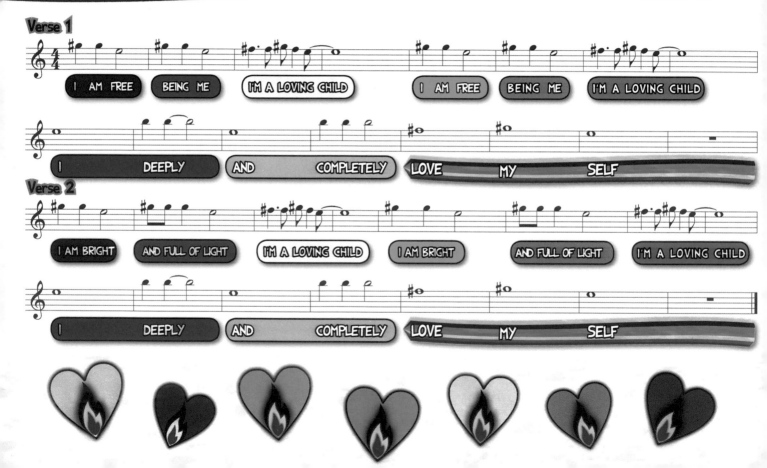

Rainbow Tuesday 2

LOVING

SIDE
OF EYE
Point 2

Rainbow Wednesday 1

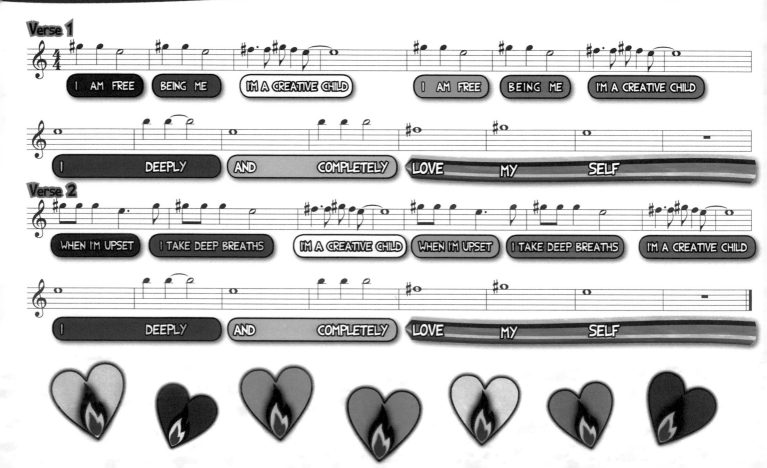

Verse 1

I AM FREE · BEING ME · I'M A CREATIVE CHILD · I AM FREE · BEING ME · I'M A CREATIVE CHILD

I · DEEPLY · AND · COMPLETELY · LOVE · MY · SELF

Verse 2

WHEN I'M UPSET · I TAKE DEEP BREATHS · I'M A CREATIVE CHILD · WHEN I'M UPSET · I TAKE DEEP BREATHS · I'M A CREATIVE CHILD

I · DEEPLY · AND · COMPLETELY · LOVE · MY · SELF

CREATIVE

WEDNESDAY 1

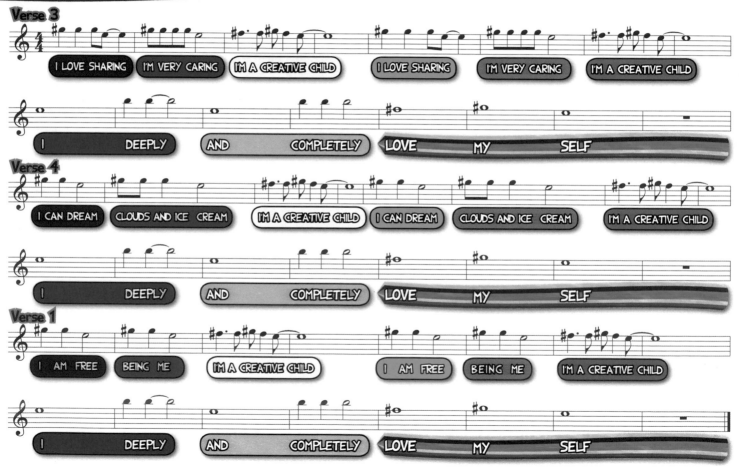

CREATIVE

UNDER
EYE
Point 3

WEDNESDAY 2

Rainbow Thursday 1

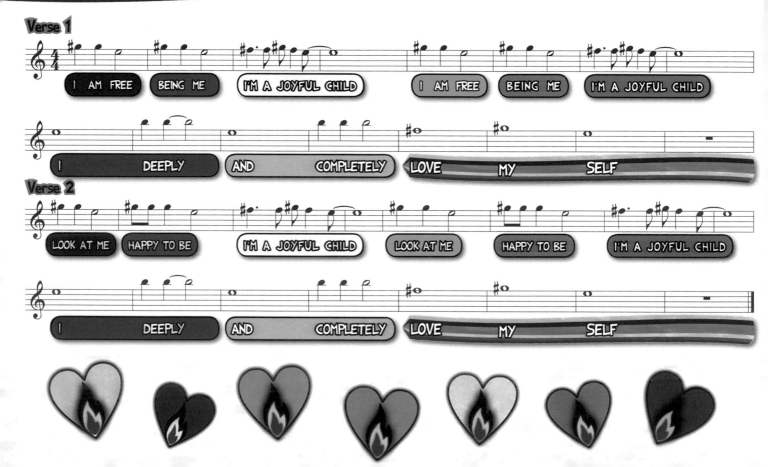

THURSDAY 1

JOYFUL

Rainbow Thursday 2

Track 4

Verse 3

IF I'M SAD · I'LL TAP TIL I'M GLAD · I'M A JOYFUL CHILD · IF I'M SAD · I'LL TAP TIL I'M GLAD · I'M A JOYFUL CHILD

I · DEEPLY · AND · COMPLETELY · LOVE · MY · SELF

Verse 4

I AM LOVED · ON EARTH AND ABOVE · I'M A JOYFUL CHILD · I AM LOVED · ON EARTH AND ABOVE · I'M A JOYFUL CHILD

I · DEEPLY · AND · COMPLETELY · LOVE · MY · SELF

Verse 1

I AM FREE · BEING ME · I'M A JOYFUL CHILD · I AM FREE · BEING ME · I'M A JOYFUL CHILD

I · DEEPLY · AND · COMPLETELY · LOVE · MY · SELF

Rainbow Friday 1

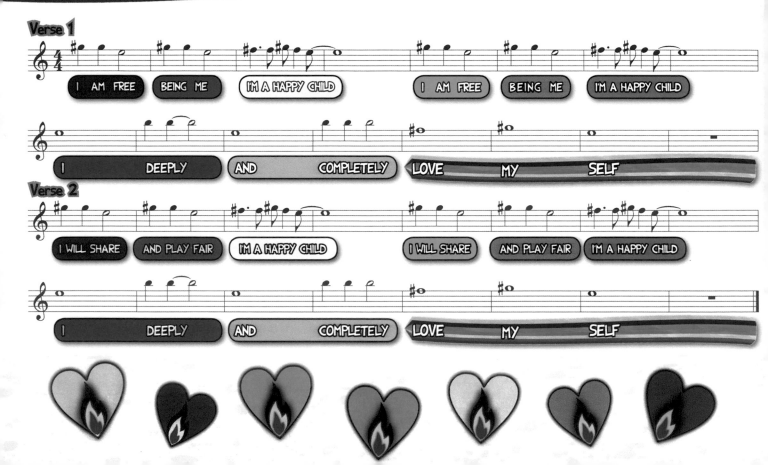

FRIDAY 1

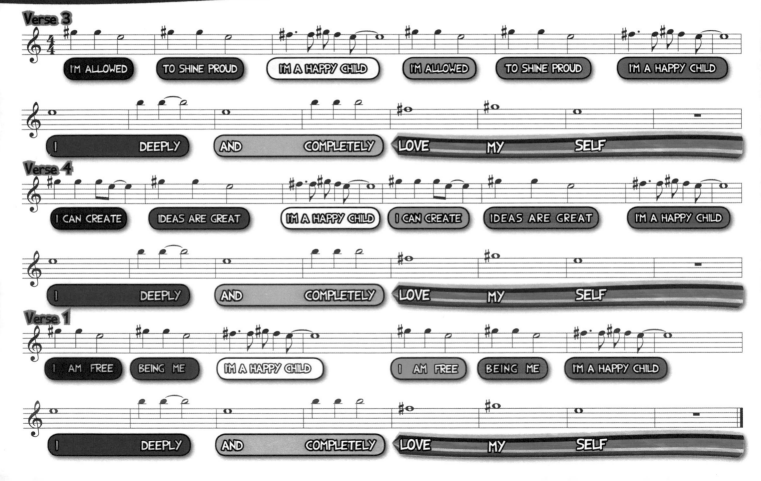

FREE BEING ME

CHIN
Point 5

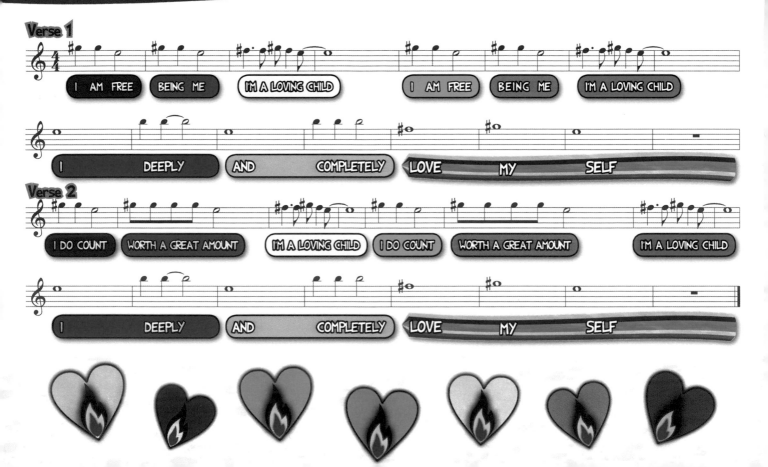

I LOVE MYSELF

SATURDAY 1

Rainbow Saturday 2

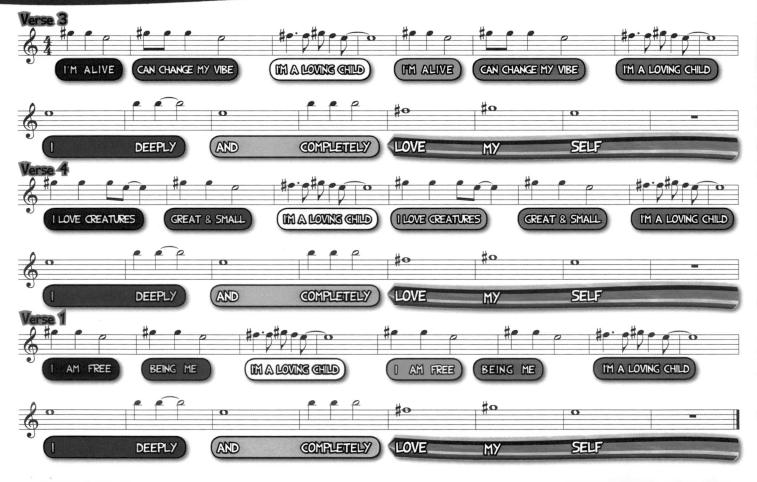

I LOVE MYSELF

COLLARBONE

Point 6

SATURDAY 2

Rainbow Sunday 1

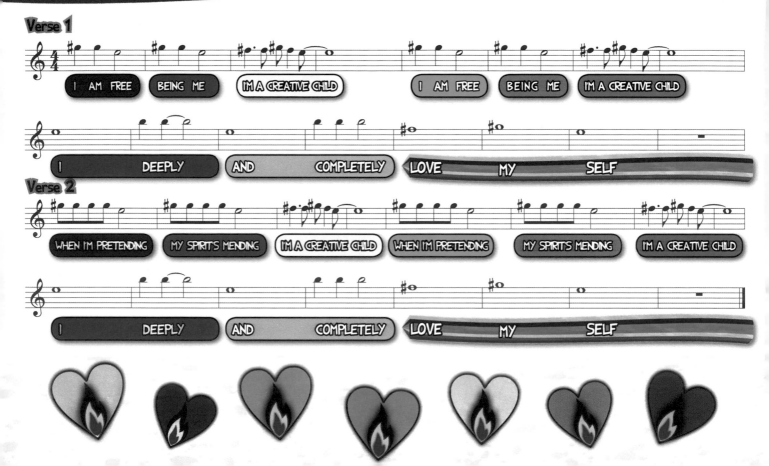

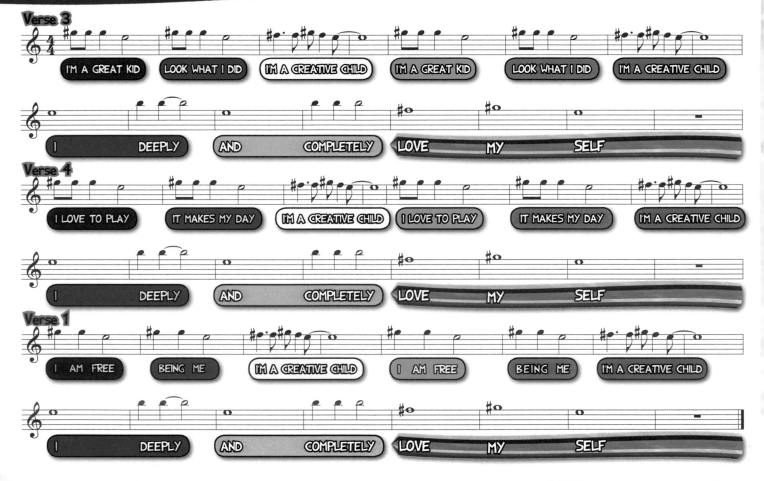

SUPER KID

UNDER ARM
Point 7

SUNDAY 2

THE TAPPING TEAM

As a creative connector and visionary, Debbie Teichmann celebrates each day with love, joy and gratitude. Debbie resides in Phoenix, AZ, and has been happily married for 36 years to her husband, Geoff. She is the mother of 3 terrific grown boys, Erik, Rob, and Tom and grandma to the new joy in her life, Westmalle. Ten years ago, Debbie, a workaholic entrepreneur stepped off her stress-filled hamster wheel onto her path of self discovery. During this beautiful journey of awakening, TAPPING PLAY was birthed and Debbie has been lovingly nurturing her new children, Annabelle, Billy and Franny. Debbie and the gang are so excited about the opportunity for families to connect through singing and tapping. To share your family's experience, learn more about Debbie or future Tapping Play books and projects go to www.tappingplay.com.

Chris Ricci grew up a fun loving child who never wanted to stop playing. Constantly trying new creative outlets he bounced around from digging sand tunnels, to building huge Lego cities, to collecting Hot Wheels and building models. Chris has always identified every event in his life by the colors that surrounded him and he eventually discovered his hidden talent for drawing and painting. This natural talent lead him to pursue Industrial and Graphic design and he received his Bachelor of Arts Degree in Design Management from Arizona State University. Chris is most influenced by oldies music & urban art. He loves designing or creating something new every day. When not playing with Annabelle, Franny and Billy, we can find Chris on the mountain slopes enjoying his other passion: Freeskiing. For more about Chris or his design services please contact him at chrisricci.design@gmail.com.

Mary Godfrey, Coach & Music Producer. started playing the keyboards at age 8, inspired by ESP Disc Recording Artist and brother, Todd Kelley. Today, Mary is a published artist, author, and producer. She is a Certified Life Coach, and has mentored many successful creative individuals and groups from A & E Writers, to Disney Performers. In the spring of 2011; Mary, along with her partners Carol, Linda, and Mollie, formed Baylight Institute for Creative Arts, LLC (B.I.C.A.) where together they help and guide the youth to find their voice through the arts while serving all ages. B.I.CA. facilitates arts instruction (Baylight Education) and production (Spicy Onion Studios). To learn more about B.I.C.A., and Mary, go to: www.BICAnow.com

Sydney Taylor, vocalist, began writing music and playing the guitar at age 9. She cut her first CD at age 11, paid for from her own "gig" money. Since then, Sydney has performed everywhere from little coffee shops, to US Airways Center (7000+), and as a featured artist on Channel 3's morning show. Now at 14, Sydney not only sings lead vocals, but sings harmony too. She plays the harp, acoustic, electric, and 12 string guitars, piano, and drums. Sydney is very interested in music production, and it's a pleasure to have her share her expressive voice with us. Expect to hear more from Sydney Taylor. In the meantime, you may contact her through her mom Laura Todd at: lauratodd@cox.net

Elmas Vincent, Consultant, plays in both the spiritual and business worlds. The seemingly disjointed events of his life prepared him to fulfill his life purpose: "Lightpreneurs" create an impact while sustaining themselves in an abundant way. His own journey includes having an entrepreneurial father, receiving an MBA from Tulane University and creating numerous successful businesses. Counter-balancing those business experiences was a continuing spiritual quest. In a class he was teaching in 2008, he first uttered the term Lightpreneurs. It has come to embrace anyone who has a business that involves making the world a better, brighter and happier place. To contact Elmas or get more information and resources please go to: www.lightpreneurs.com.

A special thanks and loving wishes to the following people who have been so supportive through my journey:

My mom (Mary), hubby (Geoff), sons (Erik, Rob and Tom), Christy, Trish, Kate, Cay, Rachel,

Marilyn, R'Delle, Michelle, Jennifer, Sandra, Barbara, Maxine,

and all my wonderful family and friends.

Made in the USA
Charleston, SC
28 November 2011